Worcester City Library

London: The Stationery Office

REFERENCE

First published 2001

ISBN 0 11 702820 7

Disclaimer

This book put YOU in control. That is an excellent thing, but it also makes YOU responsible for using it properly. Few washing machine manufacturers will honour their guarantee if you don't follow their 'instructions for use'. In the same way, we are unable to accept liability for any loss arising from mistakes or misunderstandings on your part. So please take time to read this book carefully.

This book is not a definitive statement of the law, although we believe it to be accurate and up-to-date as of 1 August 2001. We cannot except liability for changes in the law that take place after the publication date, although every effort will be made to show any such changes on the website.

Contents

About the author

Rosy Border has worked in publishing, lecturing, journalism and the law. She is a prolific author and adapter who stopped counting after 150 titles. Rosy and her husband, John Rabson, live in Suffolk and have a married son in Tennessee.

Welcome

Welcome to the *You Need This Book First* series.
Let's face it – the law is a maze. This book is your map
through the part of the maze that deals with taking in a
lodger. It contains everything lawyers would tell you
about this, if only they had time (and you had the
money to pay them). If you follow our advice you
should end up with an agreement which

● does what you want it to do

● is fair to both you and your lodger

● is legally sound

● you as a non-lawyer can understand.

Acknowledgements

A glance at the *Useful Contacts* section will show how many organisations we consulted while compiling this book. Thank you, everyone. I would particularly like to thank John Rabson, Chartered Engineer, for his IT support, research and refreshments.

We put you in control

This book

- provides the general information that professional advisers would give you on the subject, if only they had the time to do so, and if only you had the money to pay them

- tells you the buzzwords which are important in this section of the law and what they mean

- provides a plain English lodger agreement to meet most needs

- answers some of the most frequently asked questions on the subject

- helps you to keep good records of your transactions with your lodger

- is supported by a website that is regularly updated.

This book empowers you. That is a good thing; but it means responsibility as well as power. Think of yourself as a driver using a road map. The map tells you the route, but it is up to you to drive carefully.

Power points ─────────────────

Sometimes we pause to empower you to do something: watch out for the symbol.

Hazard signs

 — *We tell you when you are in danger of getting out of your depth and need to take professional advice. Watch out for the hazard sign.*

Clear English rules OK

We provide WYSIWYG documents – *w*hat *y*ou *s*ee *is w*hat *y*ou *g*et.

Legal documents have traditionally been written in archaic language, because this wording has stood the test of time – often several centuries – and has been hallowed by the courts. This language – call it lawspeak if you like – enables specialists to express esoteric concepts in a kind of professional shorthand that is clear to them but meaningless to others.

For example:

Lawyer 1: So he said to me 'This is a clear case of *'De minimis non curat lex* when he really meant *caveat emptor'*.

Lawyer 2 falls about laughing.

Lawyer 1 (wistfully): You know, for some reason I hardly know anyone who isn't a lawyer.

Lawyer 2: Me neither.

The use of lawspeak outside gatherings of lawyers is unnecessary and may be dangerous. The worst problem is that for non-specialists lawspeak is a foreign language, unknown at worst and imperfectly understood at best, with all the potential for misunderstanding which that entails. Why write agreements in a foreign language in preference to plain English? What is important is that your agreement with your lodger is expressed in clear, unambiguous language that accurately reflects your intentions.

On the (fairly rare) occasions when we *do* need to use technical language, we offer clear explanations: see *Buzzwords* on page 4.

Check out our website

Check out our website – because buying this book gives you the right to use our exclusive readers' website.

www.youneedthisfirst.co.uk

Buzzwords

HMO – house in multiple occupation: typically a large house split into several flats or bedsits.

landlord – (in this context) the householder in the property where a lodger lives in return for rent (see below). The word is unisex – there are lots of female landlords.

lodger – someone who lives with you in your own home, or in a part of the same building as you, in return for a weekly or monthly rent.

serve – lawspeak for sending or handing over a legal document.

statutory – laid down by law (statute) and therefore obligatory.

Frequently asked questions

When I was in lodgings as a student there was no **written agreement and everything went just fine. Why are you so insistent on formal contracts?**

How do you know that your landlord did not have a formal contract with your university accommodation officer? Contracts are important because

- they lay down the ground rules from the start

- they protect both you and your lodger if anything goes wrong

- some people may need reminding about what they promised to do and not to do.

I am on Income Support. Would taking in a lodger **affect my benefits?**

Almost certainly. Your income from your lodger – *which it is a criminal offence not to declare* – will be taken into account when your benefits entitlement is assessed. In some districts where there is a severe accommodation shortage, however, people on benefits are encouraged to find out whether they would still come out on top if they took in a lodger. In Essex, for example, the Harlow Accommodation Project advertises free advice and even helps with deposit guarantees. Call your local benefits office (look in the telephone directory under Benefits Agency) to see how taking in a lodger would affect your benefits. You could still come out on top.

—I am taking in a lodger who will pay a monthly rent. Do I need to provide a rent book?

No, you don't. Rent books are obligatory only if the rent is payable *weekly*. You are of course free to provide a rent book if you wish (see my suggestions on page 61). AND you will of course still have to keep good records of payments. Give your lodger a receipt for each month's rent (you will find a sample receipt on page 80 and on the website) and keep copies on file.

—Can I charge what rent I like?

For a lodger who is not on benefits, the answer is yes. In practice, of course, you are unlikely to command more than the going rate for your district and type of accommodation. Rent is a matter to be agreed between you and your lodger; and if you find someone willing to pay over the odds, good luck to you. But there might be tax to pay if your gross rent exceeds £4,250 in the tax year. See *A present from the taxman* on page 56.

If you take in a lodger on benefits, the local authority, who have guidelines to follow, may not pay as much as a private lodger would. In theory you could charge the going rate and ask the lodger to make up the shortfall, but how likely would you be to get your money?

Can I charge whatever deposit I like?

Deposits are to be decided between you and your lodger, but in general one or two months' rent would be reasonable. See *Deposits* on page 52.

I am thinking of taking in two young ladies in a twin-bedded room. Am I allowed to do this, or does each lodger have to have their own room?

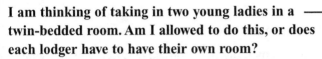

The answers are yes and no, respectively. Sharing is a matter for you to agree with your lodgers, who would obviously want some say in the choice of roommates. If your girls are happy sharing a room, that's fine.

A young unmarried couple would like my double room. Am I allowed to take them in as lodgers?

The law is silent on what my father used to call 'mixed bathing' and it is entirely up to you to decide whether or not you want this couple in your home. How stable does their relationship seem? If they part company you may be put in an uncomfortable position – can the remaining lodger afford to pay the whole rent, or will you have to ask them to leave too? – but this is a human relations problem, not a legal one.

Does my lodger's accommodation have to have its own lock and key?

The law is silent on this subject. This is something for you and your lodger to decide between you.

Will I have to pay tax on my income from my lodger?

Not unless your gross income from your lodger is more than £4,250 in a given tax year (see *A present from the taxman* on page 56 for details).

 Who is responsible for cleaning my lodger's room?

This is something to be agreed between you and your lodger. A common arrangement is for the landlord to see to the cleaning of shared areas such as the kitchen, bathroom, landing, etc., while the lodger keeps their own room clean and tidy – in which case, show them where you keep the vacuum cleaner and dusters!

 Have I any control over my lodger's visitors and how long they stay?

This is a matter for you to agree with your lodger at the beginning. It's your home and you can set the house rules. Our agreement makes no restrictions but makes your lodger responsible for any nuisance or damage caused by their visitors.

 How much notice do I have to give my lodger if I want them to leave?

If you share essential accommodation (such as a bathroom or kitchen) with your lodger, there is no legal minimum period. Otherwise the legal minimum is four weeks. In practice you should give four weeks to be both safe and friendly and the contract on page 65 reflects this.

Someone once told me that unless I provided food **my lodger would be classed as a tenant and I wouldn't be able to evict him or her without taking them to court. Is that true?**

Not if you are a resident landlord. Read *What is a lodger?* on page 11–12. And if you are not a resident landlord you are reading the wrong book.

If I died while my lodger was in residence, could the **lodger claim the right to stay on?**

The sample lodger agreement on page 65 enables whoever takes over from you to step into your shoes as landlord and enforce the agreement in your place.

I am thinking of making some alterations to my **house to provide extra facilities for my two lodgers. Do I need planning permission for this?**

The answer is a definite maybe. It is a matter of scale; if you stray into HMO territory (see *Buzzwords* and page 29) you may have to satisfy certain statutory requirements. Call your local authority for advice.

Is there any insurance I can take out against rent arrears?

Yes, there is; and it may or may not be worth your while to take it out. Consult your local insurance broker, or check out one of the numerous insurance websites (see also *Are you insured?* on page 31).

—**If my lodger has a television in his room, will he need a licence?**

Your own television licence covers all the sets in your home; and in general a lodger will be sharing your home. Of course, if you yourself have no television and your lodger brings one in, a licence will be needed and it is up to you and your lodger to agree whom should buy it.

 —**I live alone and receive a 25% reduction in my council tax on account of this. Will taking in a lodger mean I have to pay more council tax?**

There is no short answer to this, because some lodgers, such as students, would not attract council tax. And a lodger who pays council tax elsewhere (as might be the case with someone working away from home) gets special treatment. Call the council tax department of your local authority.

 —**What happens if a lodger harasses me or a member of my family?**

It depends how serious the incident is. Physical violence and racial abuse are, of course, police matters. Most local authority housing departments can advise landlords: call your local council and ask. Meanwhile, you don't have to put up with harassment in your own home. Serve your lodger with the notice to quit that you will find on page 75.

Before you take in a lodger

What is a lodger?

A lodger is someone who lives with you in your own home, or in a part of the same building, in return for a weekly or monthly rent.

It is common for lodgers to have a room of their own but to share other rooms such as the landlord's bathroom, lavatory, kitchen, etc. Some lodgers receive services from the landlord – cleaning, laundry, meals and so on – as part of the deal. Many do not; and the absence of meals or services does not stop someone from being a lodger. The key issue here is *whether or not the landlord is resident* – living under the same roof as the lodger.

People renting self-contained accommodation, such as a bedsitter, can still be lodgers as long as

● the landlord lives in the same building

● the building is the landlord's only or main home and is not, for example, a purpose-built block of flats with the landlord occupying one flat and the lodger/tenant another.

If, according to this definition, you are a resident landlord, read on. If you are not a resident landlord, you are at the wrong party. You need our *Letting Your Property* book in this series.

Although the law gives considerable protection to the tenants of *non-resident* landlords, lodgers – that is, people renting accommodation in the homes of *resident* landlords – are in a less favourable position. For example, it is much easier for a landlord to get a lodger to leave than to evict a tenant (see page 63).

Who becomes a lodger?

There are many reasons for living in lodgings rather than renting or buying a home of your own. For some people the obvious attraction is the absence of a minimum stay. An assured shorthold tenancy, which is the agreement under which most houses and flats are let, specifies a minimum period of at least six months. During that period the tenant is obliged to pay rent even if they do not occupy the premises at all. There are many people – contractors, for example – who do not know where they will be or what they will be doing in six months' time and therefore cannot realistically take on such a commitment. Here are just a few examples of people who become lodgers by choice or through force of circumstances. You can probably think of several more for yourself.

Harry, a 34-year old scaffolder, has been offered a lucrative contract 100 miles from home. He is not sure

how long the job will last, so he cannot realistically
sign an assured shorthold tenancy agreement to rent a
flat. He needs lodgings near his work and will go home
to his wife and children at weekends.

Jason, aged 18, has a job as a trainee garage mechanic
and attends college on day release. He lived at home
until his father's new wife delivered an ultimatum,
'Either Jason leaves – or I do'. Jason's own mother has
also remarried and lives a long way away. Staying with
her would mean Jason giving up his job and studies.
He can't afford to rent a flat of his own. Lodgings are
the answer.

Paula, aged 23, has just started a new job 200 miles from
her parents' home. She hopes, if all goes well, to buy a
home of her own eventually. Meanwhile she decides to
stay in lodgings while she gets her bearings, checks out
the local rent situation and starts saving for a deposit.

Edward, aged 42, has just gone through a miserable
divorce and come out of it with very little. His ex-wife
and their children live in the former family home and
Edward is keeping up the mortgage and paying
maintenance for the children. He needs lodgings on a
short-term basis while he looks for somewhere cheap
to rent.

Patrick, aged 28, has epilepsy, which is controlled by
medication. He can lead a normal life and normally
works, but is currently unemployed. His Housing
Benefit and other entitlements are not enough to make

rented accommodation in his locality an option, but lodgings are a possibility.

Sarah, aged 18, will shortly be going to university a long way from home. She didn't get a place in a hall of residence and she needs lodgings near the campus.

Whom should you avoid as a lodger?

Forget the clichés – there are exceptions to every rule except one. *Never take in friends and relations!* You of course will know the individuals better than I do; but ask yourself:

- Can I put the transaction on a businesslike footing and keep it that way?

- Can I be as firm with them as with a stranger, such as insisting on regular rent payments and observance of house rules?

- Can I be sure of getting rid of them when the time comes?

Unless the answer to all three questions is a resounding YES, find a good excuse for turning them down without hurting their feelings.

Are you allowed to take in lodgers?

Before you read any further, you need to be sure that you have the right to take in a lodger:

- If you are an owner-occupier, and you own your home outright (that is, without a mortgage), the answer is generally yes (but see *leasehold* property, below).

- If you are an owner-occupier, but there is a mortgage on the property concerned, the Department of the Environment, Transport and the Regions (DETR) advises you to ask your mortgage lender's permission before taking in a lodger. By way of research, I called three building societies, each of which said they would always say 'yes' but appreciated being asked.

- If your home is leasehold (most flats are leasehold), whether it is mortgaged or not, you must check the terms of your lease.

If your lease says you need the ground rent landlord's permission, you *must* get it before taking anyone into your home. If you do not do so, you will be contravening the terms of your lease, which is a serious matter and in a worst-case scenario could lose you your home.

● If you are a secure council tenant, as opposed for example to a council tenant in temporary accommodation, you have the right to take in a lodger. This is spelled out clearly in the DETR booklet *Your Rights as a Council Tenant – the Council Tenants' Charter* (no. 95 HCa 006, available free from the DETR – see *Useful Contacts*). It would be sensible to get yourself a copy and check that the rules apply in your case.

● If you are a tenant of a housing association, the answer is probably yes, but housing association rules differ and you should check with your own housing association before taking in a lodger.

● If you are a private tenant, the answer depends on the terms of your tenancy agreement – and in many cases on your landlord's goodwill. Check your tenancy agreement, and talk to your landlord if you are not sure. Your landlord may well ask for reassurance about insurance (see page 31) before agreeing.

Why are you doing this?

There are many possible reasons for taking a lodger into your home. All the examples below are genuine and come from my own experience. If you find them tedious, you can skip them and go on to the next section.

Financial necessity

Many people take in lodgers to make ends meet. They have a spare room and the lodger's rent helps with the rent or mortgage, the heating and other household bills. Realistically speaking, these landlords probably cannot afford *not* to share their home.

As a student in the 1960s I spent a miserable academic year as the lodger of a sour old widow in a dark, shabby but morbidly clean council house. She allowed me one bath a week (luckily there were showers in the Students' Union facilities), bolted the front door at 10 p.m. and banned all visitors of either sex. Mrs Thorn considered all students lazy, shiftless and immoral and said so, loudly and often. She felt free to enter my room without knocking and frequently, when I was out, took it upon herself to tidy my desk and inspect my cupboards and drawers for evidence of untidiness.

I thought her a joyless old harpy at the time, but I pity her now. Her only son lived in Australia, she had never seen her grandchildren and she was so grindingly poor that the income from her lodgers, far from representing a ticket to Sydney, meant the difference between paying her way and asking for handouts from the State.

It was a matter of symbiosis. We did not like each other any more than a tick bird likes a rhinoceros, but we needed each other. Mrs Thorn needed me for the money I brought in, and I needed her because I had had my permitted two years in Hall and lodgings were

scarce, good lodgings doubly so. My parents
considered a little hardship character-building – they
were probably right – and refused to intervene.
So Mrs Thorn and I served our time in sullen silence.

Space to spare

Other people – empty-nesters, perhaps – find the
family home has become too large for their current
needs. It seems a pity to let all of that space go to
waste, and the money would come in handy. That was
the reason why my husband, John, and I took in a
colleague while he house-hunted.

I modelled my style on Mrs King's – see
Companionship, below – and set ground rules that were
fair to everyone. Griff was the perfect lodger – quiet,
clean, considerate and willing to feed the cat when we
went on holiday – and we hope we were good
landlords. The relationship was pleasant but slightly
formal and we did not become friends until Griff had
moved into a place of his own. We paid no tax on
Griff's rent (see *A present from the Taxman* on page 56)
which enabled us to repaint the outside of the house.

Companionship

Some landlords are just lonely… I spent my final year
as the cherished and cosseted only lodger of an elderly,
childless widow. Mrs King lived in a large, well-
appointed house and was comfortably off. She was a
companionable soul, who liked, as she put it, 'the
sound of a key in the lock and a friendly voice in the
hall'. She had taken in lodgers – always girls in their
final year of studies – for many years and kept
photographs of her favourites on her sideboard ('All my
young people do well').

Mrs King was kind and friendly, but she laid down the
same house rules that a mother might set for a grown-
up daughter. I had my bath in the morning and she had
hers at night. I could use the kitchen before she got up
in the morning and after she had had her high tea in the
evening. I had my own shelf in the fridge, and Tuesday
was my day to use the washing machine. No radio or
record players after 10 p.m., except with headphones.
Visitors were welcome, provided they were quiet and
considerate. (No mixed bathing, of course; this was
1965!)

My space was mine. She knocked before entering and
never went in if I was not there. I called her Mrs King
and she called me Rosemary. The relationship was full
of slightly distant affection and mutual respect.
Mrs King attended my graduation and, several years
later, my wedding.

A stranger in your home

Whatever your motives for taking in a lodger, you must realise that having other people living in your home and sharing facilities is a rather intimate thing. There is a subtle alteration in the atmosphere. It goes too far to say, 'your home's no longer your own', but you are no longer alone in your home. Someone will walk on your carpets, use your loo, and possibly cook on your stove. Will it bother you?

You may be like Mrs King and actively seek company; but I know several people who have lived alone for a while, who find it very hard to contemplate taking in even the quietest and most considerate of lodgers. People like this would rather be short of money than share their home. There will be someone else living under their roof and invading their personal space; and, however harmonious their relationship with the other person, they feel uncomfortable about it. If this thought really worries you, consider taking on a paper round before you take in a lodger!

It is of course much easier for everyone if you and your lodger each have personal space. John and I were able to offer our lodger a large spare bedroom that already contained a wash basin. It did not cost much to equip it as a bedsit. We provided an electric kettle, a toaster, a small fridge, a microwave and some basic crockery and cutlery. We had two bathrooms, so there were no bottlenecks for the bog. Griff had his own day for the washing machine. We did not bother one another much.

What you yourself can offer by way of private facilities depends of course on the size and layout of your home. The amount of adaptation you are able to do will depend on whether you own your home or rent it.

The DETR leaflets suggest that before making any alterations to your home you will, even if you are an owner-occupier, want to check with your local authority. You are, however, unlikely to have any problems if all you are doing is making one or two lodgers more comfortable. When I called my local council before Griff arrived, the official said kindly, 'A wash basin in the corner of a bedroom doesn't make a bathroom and a microwave does not make a kitchen. You aren't in the HMO league yet, my dear.'

Duties and responsibilities

It is crucial not to lose sight of the legal side. Both you and your lodger will have duties and responsibilities and it is important to spell those out at the very beginning. As Mrs King would have said, 'Then we'll both know where we are, dear, and neither of us will take liberties … I've made too many scones. Would you like a couple?'

This book sets out those duties and responsibilities in an agreement that is fair both to you and to your lodger. It will also alert you to the possible problems and pitfalls on the way.

Let's start with a very important question:

Is your property habitable?

You and your family may be living quite happily in a property that is gently crumbling around you and majors in rats and cockroaches, flammable furniture and dodgy wiring. It's your home, and within reason how you keep it is your affair.

'An Englishman's home is his castle' is a popular proverb based on the writings of the great jurist Sir Edward Coke (1552–1634) who said, 'The house of everyone is to him as his castle and fortress, as well for his defence against injury and violence as for his repose'.

The law is unlikely to take much interest in your home unless it catches fire or someone actually complains to the public health department that your home is a health hazard. But as soon as you invite a lodger into your home, the law – theoretically at least – swings into action to protect your lodger from harm.

That is because someone other than you or your family has walked across the drawbridge of your castle. That someone is your lodger, and that someone has rights. From an ordinary householder, you are suddenly transformed into a landlord. As a landlord, you have a statutory duty (see *Buzzwords*) – a duty that you cannot dodge, even if your lodger is on your side – to provide your lodger with accommodation that is

- safe, especially from fire risks
- fit to live in
- free from serious disrepair.

In more detail, this means

- the property must be weatherproof and free from damp
- it must be free from vermin and insect infestation
- the electrical wiring must be safe
- any gas appliances must be safe
- there must be access to a wash basin, bath (or shower) and lavatory
- there must be adequate heating, lighting and ventilation
- flats and bedsits must have adequate means of escape in case of fire
- furniture, such as sofas, in the accommodation the lodger uses must be flame-retardant.

If you find this list daunting, you need to ask yourself whether – quite apart from your statutory duties – it is morally acceptable to ask anyone to live in accommodation which is dirty, badly equipped, cold or even dangerous. In any case, help is available. See *Power points* below.

Power points

1. If you are not sure whether your home is electrically safe, you can arrange a free electrical safety check. Contact your own electricity supplier in the first instance (there should be a display advertisement in your local telephone directory). It should be able to give you a freephone number to call.

2. Poorly maintained gas appliances cause many deaths every year. If you use gas in your home, you should for your own peace of mind get your appliances checked regularly for safety even if you do not take in a lodger. If you do take in a lodger you have a statutory duty under the Gas Safety (Installation and Use) Regulations 1998 to get your gas appliances checked for safety every year. You must use a proper CORGI (Council of Registered Gas Installers) registered fitter, who will issue you with two copies – one copy for you, one for your lodger – of a landlord's gas safety certificate.

Note that *all* gas installations in your home – not just in the parts of your home which are occupied by your lodger – must be checked for safety every year.

To find your local CORGI fitter call 01256 372300.

3. If your home is seriously substandard in some way, you might qualify for a grant. There are grants to provide essential facilities such as bathrooms for homes that have none. There are government initiatives to help make homes more energy efficient and a great deal of public money is up for grabs. Provision, and the way schemes are administered, vary from region to region. Call your local Citizen's Advice Bureau and ask what is available in your area.

4. For vermin or insect infestation, contact your local authority. Some charge for their services, but many don't. There is no need to feel embarrassed; we know of a flea invasion – bitten ankles, no less – caused by a stray cat. The same cat brought home several live mice that escaped and set up home behind the skirting board. The pest control man said both problems were very common.

5. Call in your local fire prevention officer to check your home for fire risks (see page 31 for details).

6. You have probably read terrifying tales of foam furniture bursting into flames, or giving out poisonous smoke. The same foam is perfectly safe if it is treated to make it flame-retardant. Laws were passed to outlaw untreated foam furniture, and now all new items must have been treated. The law does nothing to prevent you from filling your own home with dangerous furnishings, but it does protect lodgers and tenants. The Furniture (Fire Safety) Regulations 1993 require all sofas, chairs, mattresses and other soft furnishings in rental accommodation to be flame-retardant. For more detailed information call your local Trading Standards department.

—If you are considering buying some second hand
furniture for your lodger's room, you will be breaking
the law unless it is flame retardant. Turn the item
upside down and look for the label. A typical label –
this one came off a sofa – will say something along the
lines of

'*CARELESSNESS CAUSES FIRE*

—
*This item does not require Section 3 interliner.
All foams, fillings and composites have been tested
by our suppliers to ensure compliance with the
relevant ignitability test. Covers and fillings are
cigarette resistant. Covers are match resistant.
Further details are available from your retailer.'*

Don't buy unless there is a label. The regulations have
been around for a long time and there should be plenty
of safe items around.

—If you let 'unfit' property – property that does not meet
the statutory requirements – you can get into serious
trouble. If the worst happens and someone dies or is
injured through your negligence or carelessness, you
can be sued.

Having provided accommodation that meets the
statutory requirements, you must then keep it that way
throughout your lodger's stay (unless, of course, the
lodger causes the damage).

Habitable – and attractive

Apart from being 'habitable' in the legal sense, the
accommodation you give your lodger needs to combine
attractiveness – is it fair to offer anyone
accommodation you yourself would not like to occupy?
And besides, who would want to pay good money to
live there? – with durability.

Consider ease of maintenance, and look to the long
term.

- Choose floor covering which will wear well and
  keep its good looks for a long time. Very cheap
  floor coverings are a false economy because they
  will soon get shabby.

- Keep the décor simple, inexpensive and fairly
  neutral. You and your lodger may not share the same
  tastes! Emulsion paint is better than Colefax and
  Fowler wallpaper.

- Either have an agreement with your lodger ('You
  may put up pictures and posters provided you make
  good with filler and paint before you leave') or put
  up some old-fashioned picture rail from a DIY shop
  to enable your lodger to put up pictures without
  damaging your walls.

- Provide the best bed you can afford. You may never
  have slept in your spare bed, and your visitors may
  have been too polite to tell you how uncomfortable
  it is. The small ads are a good source of nearly new
  beds as well as other furniture.

- Thoroughly launder duvets and pillows, or buy new ones. Avoid feather fillings; many people are allergic to them.

- Charity shops are a good source of nearly new bed linen and curtains. Choose fairly neutral, inoffensive designs.

- A desk or computer work-station is a must, together with a suitable chair. Once again, check out the small ads.

- Provide plenty of space for books.

- Provide plenty of storage space for clothes, etc. A bed with drawers underneath is useful if you are short of space.

- Always buy small electrical items such as kettles, toasters, bedside lamps, etc., new to avoid potential accidents.

- Good lighting is important, especially if your lodger spends a lot of time at a desk.

I know landlords who make a point of spending 24 hours in their letting accommodation to make sure that nothing is missing (desk or table for writing? bookshelf? bedside lamp?) and that everything works. It saves time and trouble in the long run.

Multiple occupation

In general, few local housing authorities would take an interest in an ordinary house with one or two lodgers living *en famille*. In areas where there is a heavy demand for accommodation – such as in university towns – they do not want to rock the boat. In fact, a senior official (who asked not to be named) begged me not to advise my readers to ask for an inspection just for a lodger or two.

> *There's a crying need for lodgings hereabouts and we don't want the supply to dry up. Plus we're short staffed and very busy sorting out the **really** dodgy accommodation. If you asked us to inspect, we'd have to do everything by the book and pay attention to things you'd never worry about in an ordinary home.*

But if you take in more than three lodgers the local authority could take the view that you are running an HMO (see *Buzzwords*) – a house in multiple occupation. A typical HMO could be a largish house divided into several bedsits or flats, each occupied by a different individual or family. HMOs are subject to health and safety restrictions that do not apply to ordinary one-family homes.

The law has little to say about resident landlords and their lodgers. HMOs, however, are covered by regulations, the Housing (Management of Houses in Multiple Occupation) Regulations 1990 and also the Housing Act 1990. Local authorities have a statutory obligation to operate registration schemes for HMOs and to make sure the law is obeyed.

The landlord or manager of a house in multiple occupation is responsible for repairing, maintaining and cleaning the public areas of the property, organising refuse disposal and keeping the gas, electricity, drains and water supplies in good order. Safety – especially fire safety – measures are obligatory too.

Shared housing is obviously a greater fire risk than single-family housing – think of several separate kitchen stoves, apart from anything else – and the local authority will insist you install whatever fire precautions their inspector judges necessary. These will probably include smoke alarms, fire extinguishers, special door closures, fire escapes and other fire safety measures to protect the residents from risk of death or injury; and signs showing escape routes in case of fire must be on display.

There must also be a notice on display where all the residents can see it, showing the name, address and telephone number of the person managing the HMO.

Councils will also be concerned about possible overcrowding and will set a limit on the number of people allowed to live in the property.

If you think this might conceivably apply to you, speak to your local housing department at the outset, rather than risk falling foul of them later. Local authorities are

happy to advise landlords free of charge and will know
from the description that you give whether or not you
have strayed into HMO country.

Even if you are totally sure you are not about to run an
HMO, you should still consider asking your local fire
prevention officer (whose number will be in your local
telephone directory) to check out your home for fire
safety. This service, which is available to all
householders, whether owner-occupiers or tenants, will
normally be available free of charge. The FPO will
probably let you have a written report. Read it carefully
and act on it. A fire blanket by the kitchen stove and a
smoke alarm on the landing cost very little – some
local fire departments even provide them free of charge
– and could save lives.

Are you insured?

Your insurers – both buildings and contents – will want
to know what you are up to. Tell them in writing that you
are planning to take in a lodger, and keep a copy. You
will find a sample letter on page 77 and on our website.

Don't take in a lodger until you have your insurers'
go-ahead. If you do not tell your insurance company,
they may be able to refuse to pay out on a claim, such
as a fire caused by your lodger's negligence.

Your lodger's deposit will not go far if they burn your
house down!

Your lodger may want to take out insurance for his/her own possessions, especially valuable items such as computers, hi-fi equipment, etc. You may be able to combine this with your own home contents insurance policy: ask your insurers what deals are available.

—The good news: some insurers will give you a discount on your premiums if you ask the crime prevention officer from your local police to advise on security in your home, then put in place the measures he advises. These might include deadlocks on doors, a security light over the front door and window locks (which are cheap to buy and ridiculously simple to install). The advice is free, and you sometimes get a special deal on the equipment too.

This advice of course applies whether you take in a lodger or not.

—The bad news: some contents insurance policies have in their small print a fiendishly cunning get-out clause which means you will not be compensated for theft from your property unless entry has been forced. The insurance company may therefore be able to avoid paying out in the event of theft by your lodger (who of course has a key!). The moral is of course to choose your lodger with care; but the risk is still there.

—As well as protection against any damage your lodgers may do, you may also need insurance against claims by lodgers that may arise if they are injured as a result of defects in your property or contents. A loose piece of stair carpet could cost you dearly. Check your insurance policy carefully – most ordinary household policies will cover this situation. The buzzword is *third party liability.*

Finding a lodger

Most people do this for themselves. Three likely sources are

University/college accommodation offices

They may well be looking for accommodation for staff and researchers as well as students – ask. In any case, they are likely to keep a central register of property, often using a computer. Adding your name to their database is usually free – though do check this before you go ahead. The student accommodation office may have a notice board where you can pin a postcard, and the accommodation officers may be willing to pass on a handout of your details. (But take care how much information you give out – see below.)

Some universities or colleges inspect prospective lodgings before they put you on their list, others are simply glad of another address to hand out to clients.

Hospitals

There never seems to be enough accommodation for nurses and doctors and, as with universities and colleges, there will probably be an official who will be glad to add you to their database. See above.

Personnel (or human resources, or whatever they're calling them this week) departments of big employers in your area

These will usually be delighted to put you on their database or display a card on their notice board. Many will want short-term accommodation for employees who are new to the area. Industries with highly mobile workforces are a prime target.

It is sometimes possible to have an arrangement with one of these organisations, rather than with an individual lodger. In that case, the accommodation office would be responsible for the rent and you would liaise with them, not with your lodger, over any points that arose. It isn't possible to generalise; you will need to call the organisation concerned and ask whether they do such things.

Other ways of finding a lodger include

● word of mouth (but avoid close friends and relations – see the warning on page 14)

● the local housing authority

● an advertisement in a newspaper or magazine read by the kind of person you hope to attract

● the 'accommodation wanted' section of the local newspapers and free sheets

● cards in shop windows or on supermarket notice boards.

Planning your advertising

Advertisements in a local newspaper or magazine (national ones would cast your net too wide) can be expensive, but you do reach a larger readership. Start by looking at other people's ads in the property section of your local newspaper and noting the accepted abbreviations that will save you money.

Small ads usually give all or most of

- approximate location
- any obvious selling points (eg 'quiet', 'pte pkg', 'use of gdn' or 'nr shops')
- rent expected, adding 'exc' if your lodger will be responsible for utility bills and 'inc' if they will not
- Any special points (eg 'Refs reqd', 'Quiet N/S prof' or 'Sorry no DSS')
- Contact telephone no, box number or possibly e-mail address.

Draft an advertisement that seems OK to you – remember that this is your first contact with your potential lodgers, so waste a word or two saying how attractive your proposed accommodation is. Then call the advertising department of your chosen publication and find out:

- the deadline – if the property section of your local newspaper comes out on a Friday, you may need to submit your advertisement by Wednesday noon. Don't miss the boat.

- The cost. Some tele-salespeople are on commission and will try to sell you an elaborate package you don't need, such as a free insertion if you pay for three. One insertion in the right place, at the right time, will usually be enough.

You may be able to dictate the ad over the telephone, paying by credit card. If so, always ask them to send a copy of the invoice for your file. And be sure to spell out anything potentially confusing, and have the tele-sales girl or boy repeat the entire ad to you, especially the contact details. You can usually get a free insertion in the next issue if they goof seriously, such as getting your telephone number wrong, but their carelessness could lose you a week's rent.

When advertising in a newspaper or magazine it is a good idea to use a box number if you are not in a tearing hurry. A box number costs a little extra but avoids nuisance telephone calls.

A handout or a card for a notice board will need to be both legible and presentable. Typing or print is better than manuscript unless your handwriting is totally readable and very beautiful indeed.

A word of warning

You may be too young to have seen *The Ladykillers*, in which Alistair Sim and his gang of robbers pose as musicians to gain the confidence of their sweet, vulnerable old landlady while they plan their great coup. The film ended happily. But this is a 'wicked old world'.

Looking on the black side, we have all heard of criminals answering accommodation advertisements as part of their preparations for future burglaries. There are also some sad, unstable men who call the numbers in the small ads and, if a female voice answers, say obscene or threatening things. And there have been cases of lodgers committing criminal offences against the persons and property of their landlords. A lodger recently (May 2001) received a life sentence for murdering his landlady.

Anyone who takes in a lodger is accepting a certain amount of risk, risk that begins even before your lodger crosses the threshold.

You can at least minimise the risk by being sparing with the information you give out in any advertisements and by finding out what you can about your prospective lodger's personal history and background.

To protect yourself, consider some or all of the following:

- Be aware that not all callers may be looking for lodgings, and that some villains can be very plausible.

- Don't give your full address in any advertisement – a contact number is sufficient.

- When someone rings to enquire about your accommodation, write down whatever telephone number they give you, then ring 1471 afterwards to check that the two numbers are the same.

- Avoid giving any personal information – such as the fact that you live alone – in your advertisement or on the telephone.

- Don't answer late-night telephone calls. People can call again at a reasonable hour, or forget the whole thing.

- If the call turns obscene or malicious, resist the temptation to burst into tears (they'll love it) or make wisecracks (they'll call you again to see if you can keep it up). Just put down the receiver, do a swift 1471 in case they've been careless, and in any case tell both your telephone company and the police.

- Don't give a candidate your address until you are sure you want to meet them.

- Before meeting a candidate, always call them at home or at work, ostensibly to double-check the time of your appointment.

- Listen to your inner voice. If you don't like the sound of them, don't meet them face to face.

- Try to arrange for a friend or, if you have one, your dog to be with you when you do meet candidates. Your friend can check 'em out as well; and if your normally benign hound growls and goes all stiff-legged, ask yourself why.

Vetting your lodger

Taking in a lodger on the spur of the moment is like marrying in haste – you may find yourself repenting at leisure. Once a candidate gets past first base (see above) take time to interview them carefully. Inviting someone to live with you in your own home is a very personal matter. Do remember, however, that your potential lodgers will be checking you out too!

You are looking for someone who will

- pay the rent
- be considerate in using any shared parts of your home
- get along with you and your family.

Horror stories apart, you need to be clear in your own mind about the house rules you will set – and enforce. For example,

- would you reject a smoker out of hand?
- what about music in the evenings?
- how do you feel about visitors?

This person is going to live under your roof and you have every right to turn down anyone you find uncongenial or who you think might cause annoyance to you or your neighbours. It is sensible to write a list of all the possible areas of disagreement: you are the person best placed to do this.

I tend to sift candidates as we talk on the telephone, making notes that I keep for my file. You will find a checklist for applicants' first contact information on page 76. Use a fresh sheet of paper for each caller. It is surprisingly easy to mislay people's details unless you are organised. You may find yourself rejecting several hopefuls before you actually make an appointment to show anyone around. This is to be expected.

The interview

If you have not done much interviewing before, consider having a dry run with a friend playing the part of a prospective lodger.

Allow plenty of time for each prospective lodger. Have their first contact details in front of you (see page 76) and a list of points to mention (washing machine rights? power points/television aerial?). You might like to use the checklist on page 42 in making your own notes about the candidate.

Try to envisage the kinds of questions you are likely to be asked, and have your answers ready.

Here is a checklist of points to consider:

1 Are you prepared to accept a lodger on benefits?

See *'She was poor but she was honest'* on page 47.

2 If not, are you satisfied that your prospective lodger would be able to pay the rent?

We're not talking about demanding a complete statement of means here, just some indication that there is enough money coming in from a reliable source.

3 Has your prospective lodger got either the deposit or the means to obtain it (there are schemes to help housing benefit clients with deposits – see page 54)?

4 Is your prospective lodger likely to be clean, tidy and punctual?

I would reject out of hand anyone who turned up late for their interview without a good reason, wearing anything other than clean clothes and 'shining morning face'. The unpunctual, scruffy ones may be warm, wonderful people but I don't want to share my house with them. This is of course a matter of personal preference and you are welcome to disagree.

5 Is your prospective lodger being frank with you?

Beware of anyone who seems unwilling to talk about their employer, their previous landlord, etc. You will of course, in any case, ask for references – and follow them up. See *References* on page 45 below.

6 Remember that the rent, which you have set after carefully researching the going rates for your area, is not negotiable. If a prospective lodger wants to haggle, turn them down flat.

7 Make clear your views on things like smoking, pets, visitors, use of washing machine, kitchen rights, access to your telephone, the lodger's own electrical equipment (you could insist on an electrical safety check before letting it into your home), etc, etc and stick to your guns.

8 Is there anything about the prospective lodger that might annoy you or your neighbours? Do not, for example, accept a lodger who is learning the saxophone unless you either live in a detached house or are sure everyone in the street will appreciate the music.

9 Be businesslike, but listen to your own gut reactions too. If there seems something faintly dodgy about a prospective lodger, something you can't quite put your finger on, there is probably a good reason. Trust your intuition. You will not often be wrong.

They're checking you out too ...

Remember that while you are cautiously assessing your prospective lodger, you are being checked out too. Be ready when the doorbell rings, and make sure your home, and especially the accommodation the lodger will occupy, looks as attractive and welcoming as possible.

Some candidates may have several places to view.
You may like to give each one a small typed or printed
handout to remind them what you are offering. Include
address, rent, deposit and your contact telephone
number.

Accepting and rejecting

Never decide on the spot, however strong your gut
feeling about someone. Say 'I'll let you know', name a
day or time to call them, and keep your promise.

 Race discrimination is against the law. Even if you
draft a racially discriminatory ad, no responsible
newspaper will publish it.

Although the Discrimination Act 1995 does not apply
to resident landlords letting accommodation in their
own home, you should not turn away a prospective
lodger on grounds of race. Apart from the fact that you
might be turning down the perfect lodger, you would be
encouraging racism. Of course, there are many
perfectly acceptable reasons for turning someone down
– bad references, for example.

Be nice

In turning people down, be kind and tactful. Nobody
likes to feel rejected. Emphasise how difficult it was to
make your choice. The unsuccessful candidates will
inevitably talk to their friends and colleagues, and you
would prefer them to speak well of you …

When you call your chosen lodger to inform them of
their good fortune, you must tell them that the deal is
subject to satisfactory references – see below.

Never worry about possible loss of income if you are
slow in establishing your lodger. It is better to have a
lean couple of weeks while you seek out the perfect
lodger than to install one in haste and regret it at
leisure.

References

Once you have made your choice, it is time to do some
serious checking. However charming your prospective
lodger seems, the two key questions are always

● Can your lodger pay the rent?
● Will your lodger look after your property?

Nothing can guarantee a 'Yes' to both questions, but
you can reduce the risks by

● asking for references
● following them up
● taking a deposit (see below).

Do not rely on references that the lodger hands you.
A colleague of mine once interviewed a prospective
lodger whose glowing testimonial, supposedly from the
director of the haulage firm of which the lodger was a
transport manager, turned out to be bogus. Well, to be

precise, the headed paper was genuine, the lodger was who he said he was, but when my colleague telephoned the director he had never given such a reference. The prospective lodger had typed and signed the document himself. If my colleague had been lax about checking him out, she could have let a liar and a cheat into her house.

I suggest asking for

● a financial reference, such as from an employer (is your lodger's job secure?)

● a reference from a previous landlord (why did he/she leave?)

● a personal reference from a responsible person who has known your prospective lodger for at least three years.

Always take up the references. There is a sample reference request on page 79 and on our website. Always enclose a stamped, addressed envelope if you are expecting a reply by post.

Some referees will be more forthcoming over the telephone than in a letter: listen carefully and note any hesitation or too-careful choice of words. Nobody likes to speak ill of anyone, but there are ways of leaving things unsaid.

'Henry was – er – very gregarious', could mean that Henry held wild parties at unsocial hours.

'She was poor but she was honest' – lodgers on benefits

If you have set your heart on a fine upstanding lodger with the right connections and a well paid job, you can skip this section. Not all people on benefits are scroungers, however; and if you have ever been in difficulties yourself you may wish to help someone else who has fallen on hard times. There is a particular demand for lodgings for

● young people between 16 and 25

● divorced and separated people

● people with special needs.

There are two likely sources of potential lodgers on benefits:

● the local authority housing department

● local homelessness charities and similar organisations.

Not all areas are well served by the latter. The national homelessness organisations such as Shelter tend to be better at giving legal advice than actually finding accommodation; but there are some wonderful local initiatives, often operating on a shoestring.

In my own area the Coastal Housing Action Group works hand in hand with the local authority and benefits agencies to match landlords with prospective lodgers and tenants.

Its relationship with landlords is exemplary. It will take careful note of the landlord's requirements and can often arrange a 'beauty parade' of prospective lodgers. It will lend a hand with form filling for candidates on benefits and may even be able to provide deposits from its own funds or from related charities. It can often advance the first month's rent too, which is a thing no local authority, however helpful otherwise, is likely to do (although see page 54 about the deposit guarantee scheme).

Potential lodgers don't need to be on benefits to consult CHAG; many people in good jobs who are new to the area consult CHAG rather than an agent who may charge them extortionate fees for poor service.

To see what your local CHAG equivalent is, approach your local Citizen's Advice Bureau for details of organisations operating in you area.

Young people under 18 need special handling because they cannot make legally binding agreements. The buzzword here is 'guarantor' – an adult to guarantee that you will get paid. Ask the housing department or charity what guarantee schemes they operate – some young people are in the care of the local authority, who will act as guarantor – and if you are not satisfied with it, choose a different lodger.

Direct payment of rent

If you do take a lodger who qualifies for housing
benefit, you can (with the lodger's agreement – you will
be given a special form for you both to sign) arrange for
the rent to be paid directly to you. If a lodger on
housing benefit gets behind with the rent, the housing
authority can choose to pay you direct anyway, but as
there usually have to be at least eight weeks' arrears,
you may prefer to be paid direct from the beginning.

Note, however, that there is a potential problem (see
below).

A local authority may not pay you as much as a private
lodger would. The housing benefit it will pay out is
based on

● the lodger's age and entitlement
● what the local rent officer regards as the going rate
for the accommodation you are offering – which
may not be the same as what the private market will
bear.

The local authority is likely to ask a rent officer to
inspect your property and set the level of rent.
In theory you can expect an official with a clipboard
to knock on your door. In practice the 'inspection'
may simply be done in the office, based on a glance
at the street map of your area and the rent officer's
knowledge of the going rate for the kind of deal you
are offering.

Once this has been done, the local authority has set a
rent and your lodger has moved in, you may face a
longish wait for your money while your case works its
way laboriously through the local authority system.
I know landlords who have been kept waiting for two
months for their money while the paperwork moved
through the system. This is where the rent advance
scheme offered by some homeless charities could come
into its own. Ask about this.

Coping with officialdom

This is not a book about local authorities, but it is
worth mentioning that officials can and do lose
documents and then deny ever having received them.
This is usually due to the 'If I can't find it on the
computer system it doesn't exist' phenomenon. It can
take many working days to transfer the information on
a stack of forms onto the computer system and forms
have been known to go AWOL before their details have
been entered, and people can and do make typing
errors in transferring your information to their
database. Of course, the inconvenience for you is the
same whatever the reason for the hiccup. In your
dealings with officialdom it pays to

- open a file labelled LODGER

- make a note of any reference number or code
  allocated to your case, write this in thick black felt
  tip on the file, and quote it in every communication
  – both by telephone and in writing – with the
  authority

- keep a copy of everything you send or hand in

- keep careful notes for your file of all telephone conversations, with dates and the name of the official you spoke to. You think you will remember: believe me, in a month's time you will have forgotten all about it!

- get a signed receipt for everything you hand in

- make friends with an official connected with your case, write their name on the front of the file in thick black felt tip and call them regularly to ask about progress.

Clawing back overpayments

Having your lodger's housing benefit paid straight to you can work very well. You get the money before your lodger can spend it on riotous living. But beware! If, because of your lodger's benefit fraud, the local authority pays out more money than to which the lodger is entitled – *even if you yourself are totally unaware of anything untoward* – the local authority will claw back the overpayment from *you*.

It has the statutory power to recover this money from you and, because it is generously rewarded by central government for doing so, it will do its utmost to exercise that power.

It will do it either by demanding payment from YOU then and there or by deducting the overpayment in instalments from the ongoing rent. If you don't pay, it has the power to take you to court for the money, and recent case law indicates that it will win. A county court judgment against you would affect your future credit rating. It sure as hell ain't fair on an innocent landlord, but that's what will happen.

You are then supposed to claim the money back from your lodger, but this is stressful at best and costly at worst. Suppose you get a county court judgment against your lodger: you may never see your money. You can't get blood out of a stone. The judge will take the lodger's income into account and may order them to pay off their debt in such small instalments that you might as well have written off the money in the first place.

This is a worst-case scenario, and if you choose your lodger carefully it may never happen to you.

Deposits

It is important to ask your lodger for a deposit in addition to the first month's rent. This

- is a useful test of a private lodger's financial soundness

- reminds your lodger to behave

- gives you some protection if the lodger lets you down.

At the end of your lodger's stay, this sum can be used to cover any unpaid rent, pay the cost of cleaning the property (unless, of course, cleaning is part of the deal) and make good any damage the lodger has done.

There is no upper or lower limit set by law, but one or two months' rent would be normal. The deposit (or what is left after any deductions you have to make for repairs, cleaning, etc.) should be returned to the lodger at the end of their stay. Always give the lodger a receipt for their deposit. You will find a sample receipt on page 81 and on the website.

Remember that a deposit is the lodger's money, not yours. You might have recourse to it in future; but for the moment you can't touch it. It is wise, therefore, to put your lodger's deposit in an interest-bearing account that is separate from your own finances. Who gets the interest on the money is a matter to be agreed between you and your lodger.

I know a few saintly landlords who pick accounts that pay high interest and pass onto their departing lodgers the interest their deposits have earned, but this is of course optional. Intelligent Finance, for example, operates a high interest account that enables you to keep money in several different 'pots' with names chosen by you. You might consider opening one of these with your lodger's first name and keeping the monthly statement in your file.

Deposits for lodgers on benefits

You may think that deposits would be out of the
question for lodgers on benefits (see page 47); but you
would be wrong.

Many local authorities run a deposit guarantee scheme
for lodgers and tenants on benefits. Typically, the local
authority gives the landlord a guarantee or bond (not
actual money – see below) to cover a maximum of one
month's rent. The bond is handed to the landlord as a
deposit. In return for this, the lodger pays a small sum
– typically £5 or £10 – to the local authority and
promises

- to pay the rent promptly
- not to cause any damage
- to pay the council for any damage that is caused.

If there is any damage at the end of the lodger's stay,
the local authority – not the lodger – pays the landlord.
The local authority then tries to recover the cost from
the lodger; but meanwhile you will have had your
money.

Additionally, some housing charities can arrange
deposits either from their own funds or from other
charities. Your local Citizen's Advice Bureau will have
lists of charities operating in your area.

Ex-service charities such as Forces Help can sometimes
provide deposits for old comrades who have fallen on

hard times. They may treat the deposit as a gift to the individual, not a loan, which means that if you have to use the deposit they will not ask you for their money back.

A present from the taxman

It isn't often that the taxman gives anything away. However, the Inland Revenue's 'Rent-a-Room' scheme was designed to increase the accommodation available for renting by encouraging people to rent out spare rooms in their homes.

Previously, potential landlords were nervous of doing this in case they were landed with a big tax bill. Under the Rent-a-Room scheme they needn't worry unless they are making serious money. And landlords do not need to be owner-occupiers to claim this allowance. Council and housing association tenants are eligible too.

If your *gross* rental income – that is, your income *before expenses* – from your lodger in any one tax year – that is, from 6 April one year to 5 April the next – is not more than £4,250 (which comes to £354.16 a month or £81.73 per week), then that income is exempt from tax. If you and someone else – such as your partner – let the room jointly, you will each be entitled to half of the tax exemption – in other words £2,125.

There is a space for Rent-a-Room scheme income on your annual tax return. Unless your gross income from your lodger is more than £4,250 in the tax year concerned, all you need to do is tick the box and go on to the next section.

If your gross income from your lodger is more than £4,250, you can choose to pay tax *either*

● on your *net* profit (in other words, the gross rent less your expenses) or

● on the part of the gross rent you receive which exceeds £4,250. (So if the gross rent were £5,000 you would be liable for tax on the extra £750 at whichever rate you would normally be liable for.)

You do not, therefore, have to take part in the Rent-a-Room scheme if it is not to your advantage. Instead, you could ignore Rent-a-Room and simply declare all your income from your lodger and claim expenses and capital allowances against tax.

A free Inland Revenue leaflet, *Letting and Your Home* (IR87), available from any tax office or on the Revenue's website >www.inlandrevenue.gov.uk< explains in detail how the scheme works and how to decide whether it is for you.

Down to brass tacks

Before signing anything, you and the prospective lodger need to agree

- the amount of rent
- whether this will be paid weekly or monthly
- how it will be paid, eg cash, cheque or standing order
- whether the rent will be higher in winter to cover higher heating costs
- whether the lodger will be responsible for any utilities
- what the lodger proposes to do about insuring his or her own possessions.

(Note that our lodger agreement on page 65 and on the website contains two optional clauses – 5.7 and 5.8 – to provide for your lodger to pay for separately metered services, and council tax/water rates if the lodger's accommodation is separately assessed. If this does not apply to you, you will of course delete those clauses.)

- the amount of deposit (if any)
- the notice period – how much warning you will give the lodger if you want them to leave, and vice versa.

If you share essential accommodation with your lodger, there is no legal minimum notice period. Our agreement on page 65 and on the website gives you the option of a week, a month or three months.

Otherwise the legal minimum is four weeks. In practice you should give at least four weeks' notice to be both safe and friendly.

● the contents of the accommodation, and their condition. It is wise to produce an inventory that the lodger checks and signs (see the inventory on page 84)

● what services, if any, you will provide (eg cleaning, cooking, bed linen).

You will want to incorporate all the information above in your final agreement.

And now ...

● 'Top and tail' the agreement on page 65 to meet your needs, as above, and print out two copies.

● 'Top and tail' the inventory (see page 84) to cover the accommodation and equipment you are providing and print out two copies.

● Fill in the lodger agreement in duplicate (one copy for you, one for the lodger).

● Arrange a meeting with the lodger before he/she moves in, and at the meeting

- go through the lodger agreement and sign and date both copies of the lodger agreement

- get the lodger to sign and date both copies (if you are to have more than lodger, get everyone over 18 to sign)

- give the lodger one copy and keep the other

- go through the inventory together and get the lodger to sign both copies (one for each of you)

- give the lodger their copy of your gas safety certificate

- collect the deposit (if any) and give a receipt

- collect the first instalment of rent and give a receipt

- hand over a key.

Congratulations! You did it all by yourself!

Collecting the rent

A good lodger will pay the rent without being nagged. However, if you need to demand payment, you MUST

● do so in writing and

● put your name and address on your demand,

otherwise it will not be valid. See the sample demand on page 82 and on the website.

Rent and record books

For lodgers who pay their rent *weekly* (or if your lodger agreement refers to a weekly amount) you are required by law to provide your lodger with a proper rent book. You can get this from any good stationers. (An old exercise book won't do and looks naff anyway.)

If yours is a *monthly* agreement, you are not required by law to provide a rent book. You will of course still have to keep good records of payments.

Here is a practical way of recording payments as well as other points that arise.

Buy a hardback notebook and enter on the flyleaf the lodger's

- name
- contact telephone number
- date of arrival
- amount of rent paid in advance
- amount of deposit paid
- date when rent is next due.

Then each time your lodger pays their rent, you enter on one side of the next double page spread the date and amount of rent paid, and sign it.

On the other side you write about any points, major or minor, that have arisen during the month. ('put up new curtains/replaced broken teapot'), sign and date. Many landlords find this record very useful, especially for settling any disagreements.

Give your lodger a receipt for each month's rent (you will find a sample on page 80 and on the website) and keep copies on file. Many landlords prefer to use a personal computer to generate the receipts and keep track of payments, but a receipt book with either carbon copies or stubs like a cheque-book is just as good.

 Beware of the lodger who offers to pay you in kind.

A spot of digging, baby-sitting or DIY is fine, provided the lodger is not breaking any rules by doing so. There are strict rules about payments in cash or kind for lodgers on benefits.

Parting company

In practice, most lodgers will leave when you ask them. If your lodger tries to dig their heels in,

● serve (see *Buzzwords*) the notice to quit, which you will find, on page 75 and on the website.

If the lodger refuses to budge at the end of the notice period, you have the right to evict a lodger without taking them to court if, but only if, *you share some essential accommodation* (such as kitchen, bathroom, lavatory – corridors and staircases don't count here) *in your only or main home both when your lodger moves in and at the time when you want them to go*. Even so

● you must issue a proper notice to quit (see page 75)

● you must not use or threaten physical violence. Both unlawful eviction and harassment are criminal offences.

If you do *not* share essential accommodation with your lodger and if they refuse to budge, you may not be able to evict them without a court order. This is not a DIY matter. Take professional advice.

Moving house

If you move out of your home permanently (as opposed to going away for a few weeks on business or on holiday), you cease to be a resident landlord and your legal position changes drastically. You *must* therefore make sure your lodger leaves when you do. If not, your lodger could become your tenant and gain statutory long-term right of residence. The lodger agreement on page 65 provides for whoever takes over from you to step into your shoes and become the landlord.

If for some reason you want to leave your lodger behind when you move house, the answer is to grant them an assured shorthold tenancy (see our book *Letting Your Property* for details).

Student and holiday lettings

Students can be lodgers just like anybody else, but if, according to the criteria on page 11–12, you are a non-resident landlord, you will need our book *Letting Your Property*.

Holiday lets are a different ballgame altogether, and are not covered in this book.

Lodger agreement

Now we come to the agreement. You will see that the agreement itself is quite a short document, but it comes with a long list of Standard Provisions.

The *agreement* is specific – it is unique to you (whom we have described as the Landlord throughout) and your lodger. The *standard provisions* are more general – well, let's face it, they're standard. Because of that, there may be things in them that do not apply to your case. The *standard provisions* are important, however, because they set out the rules that you and your lodger are agreeing to abide by. It is important to read the Standard Provisions yourself, and to take time to talk them through with your lodger, before you both sign the agreement.

Lodger agreement
(original)

Date:

The Landlord: [your name and full address here]

The Lodger: [your lodger's name here]

The Accommodation: [describe the accommodation of which the lodger will have sole use]

The Contents: As set out in the attached inventory

The Shared Rooms:
[Here you list shared accommodation, e.g. kitchen, bathroom, utility room, etc; thoroughfares like hallways and staircases do not count as 'rooms']

The Rent:
£   [insert amount here]
Payable weekly/monthly in advance on the [ ] day of the week/month.

Deposit:
£   to be paid on the signing of this agreement with the Landlord.

Notice Period: 1 week/1 month/3 months [delete whichever does not apply].

A   The Landlord gives the Lodger the personal right to live in the accommodation and to use the shared rooms with the Landlord/the Landlord's family. [delete whichever does not apply]

B   The Lodger agrees to observe and perform the obligations set out in the Terms and Conditions enclosed with this Agreement.

C   This agreement can be ended at any time:

C1   By the Landlord giving the Lodger notice to quit the accommodation at the end of the notice period

C2   By the Lodger giving the Landlord notice of his/her intention to vacate the accommodation at the end of the notice period.

D   The Landlord agrees to provide the following services:
[here set out what you are prepared to offer, eg breakfast, cleaning, laundry, etc]

E   The Landlord's address for service of notices (including notices of proceedings) is the address given for the Landlord at the start of this agreement.

Signed by the Landlord ....

Lodger agreement
(duplicate)

Date:

The Landlord: [your name and full address here]

The Lodger: [your lodger's name here]

The Accommodation: [describe the accommodation of which the lodger will have sole use]

The Contents: As set out in the attached inventory

The Shared Rooms:

[Here you list shared accommodation, eg kitchen, bathroom, utility room, etc.]

The Rent:

£   [insert amount here]

Payable weekly/monthly in advance on the [ ] day of the week/month. [delete whichever does not apply]

Deposit:

£   to be paid on the signing of this agreement with the Landlord.

Notice Period: 1 week/1 month/ 3 months [delete whichever does not apply]

A   The Landlord gives the Lodger the personal right to live in the accommodation and to use the shared rooms with the Landlord/the Landlord's family. [delete whichever does not apply]

B   The Lodger agrees to observe and perform the obligations set out in the Terms and Conditions enclosed with this Agreement.

C   This agreement can be ended at any time:

C1   By the Landlord giving the Lodger notice to quit the accommodation at the end of the notice period

C2   By the Lodger giving the Landlord notice of his/her intention to vacate the accommodation at the end of the notice period.

D   The Landlord agrees to provide the following services:
[here set out what you are prepared to offer, eg cleaning, laundry, etc]

E   The Landlord's address for service of notices (including notices of proceedings) is the address given for the Landlord at the start of this agreement.

Signed by the Lodger...

Lodger agreement: standard provisions

I have added my own notes *in italics* at the end of each clause. It is sensible to talk your lodger through the agreement, referring to the notes and making sure everything is clear.

1.   Any restriction on the Lodger includes an obligation not to permit or allow an infringement by anyone visiting the Lodger.
(The agreement applies to anyone visiting the lodger as well as to the lodger him/herself.)

2. Words in the masculine are deemed to include the feminine and vice versa. The singular includes the plural and vice versa.

(This avoids using 'he/she/they', 'him/her/them', etc. I wish I could do the same! I have tended to use 'they/them/their' in lieu of 'he/she, him/her and his/her'. If this irritates you, I apologise.)

3. If there is more than one Lodger, all their obligations can be enforced against all the Lodgers jointly and against each one individually.

(If, for instance, there are rent arrears, and you have an agreement with two lodgers, neither can avoid liability by claiming to have paid their share of the rent.)

4. The Landlord includes whoever for the time being owns the interest in the Property which gives a right to possession of it when the Lodger's right of occupation ends.

(This means that if you sell the house, or die, the new owner of the house steps into your shoes and the agreement remains in force (see frequently asked questions on page 9).

5. **The Lodger shall:**

5.1 Pay the rent at the time and in the manner stated without any deduction.

(The lodger pays the amount set out in the agreement, without deductions, at the time set out in the

agreement. If you want the rent paid by standing order, you can insist on this.)

5.2 Pay for telephone calls that the Lodger makes from the Landlord's Property.
(The lodger pays for their own phone calls if they use **your** *telephone. Lodgers with mobile phones are of course responsible for their own bills.)*

5.3 Use the accommodation for the Lodger to live in and no other purpose.
(This prevents the lodger using the property for business purposes.)

5.4 Keep the accommodation clean and tidy.
(No problem.)

5.5 Leave the shared rooms clean and tidy after use.
(No problem.)

(The two clauses below may not apply to your case. See below.)

5.6 If supplies to the Accommodation are separately metered, arrange immediately with the relevant supply company for accounts for gas, electricity and telephone (if any) at the Accommodation to be addressed to the Lodger in his own name and pay all standing charges for these and all charges for gas and electricity supplied to the Accommodation and for telephone calls made from the Accommodation during the letting period.

5.7 If the Accommodation is separately assessed for Council Tax and/or water rates, pay the Council Tax and/or water rates for the Accommodation applicable for the letting period.
(Optional – these apply only when supplies are separately metered or the lodger's accommodation is separately assessed. You can omit these clauses, or cross them out and initial them, if they do not apply to you, and re-number accordingly.)

6. The Lodger shall not:

6.1 Sell, hire out or remove the Contents.
(The lodger may not sell your sofa, donate your dresser or loan out your lawnmower.)

6.2 Deface or damage the accommodation, any part of the Landlord's Property, or the Contents.
(This stops the lodger putting up shelves, hammering picture hooks into the walls or scratching the table-tops. Many landlords put up picture hooks themselves; and some agree to sticky tape provided the lodger makes good afterwards.)

6.3 Play any live or electronic music, radio or TV or engage in any other noisy activity between such hours as the Landlord stipulates.
(This covers everything noisy that might annoy you or your neighbours. 11 p.m. to 8 a.m. would be reasonable; this is something you must agree with your lodger.)

6.4   Keep anything dangerous or inflammable at the accommodation.
(No bombs, shotguns, chemistry sets, cans of petrol or portable Calor or other gas heaters.)

7.1   The Landlord holds the Deposit as security for compliance by the Lodger with his/her obligations, and the payment holding and use of the Deposit shall be without prejudice to any other right or remedy of the Landlord.
(This allows you to hold the deposit and use it as you think proper. But see our advice on page 53.)

7.2   If the Landlord shall need to have recourse to the Deposit while this agreement continues, the Lodger shall immediately on demand pay the Landlord such amount as shall be required to restore the amount of the Deposit to the original sum.
(If you need to use part of the deposit, this clause enables you to make the lodger top it up again.)

7.3   The Deposit shall be paid to the Lodger at the end of this Agreement less such part of it as the Landlord shall deem necessary to enable the Landlord to make good any breach of or non compliance with the Lodger's obligations under this agreement. If the Deposit shall be insufficient for this purpose the Lodger shall pay to the Landlord forthwith on demand such further sum as shall in the opinion of the Landlord be required.
(At the end of their stay the lodger gets the deposit back, less any that you have to spend to put right

anything the lodger has done or failed to do. If the deposit is not enough to put things right, you can make the lodger pay the difference.)

8. If at any time any part of the rent is in arrears for 15 days (whether formally demanded or not) or any of the obligations on the Lodger's part are not observed and performed the Landlord may re-enter the accommodation and this agreement shall cease and determine.

(This is fairly draconian; you would of course try a gentle reminder first!)

Signed by the Landlord . . . .

Signed by the Lodger . . . .

Other documents

Notice to quit

From: [fill in your name and address here]
('The Landlord')

To: [fill in your lodger's name here]
('The Lodger')

Date:

I refer to the agreement between us by which you occupy accommodation as my lodger. The agreement can be ended by either of us giving to the other notice of (1 week/1 month/3 months). [landlord fills in according to the period set out in the Lodger Agreement]

By this notice to quit, I require you to vacate the accommodation

on ....[date] and to leave the accommodation and the contents in the good condition which the agreement requires.

Signed by the **Landlord** ....

I acknowledge receipt of the original notice to quit of which this is a duplicate.

Signed by the **Lodger** ....

Checklist: First telephone contact with prospective lodger

Candidate's name

Where do they come from?

Contact telephone number

At work [ ]   student [ ]   on benefits [ ]

Can they give references? [ ]

Deposit available? [ ]

Any other information they offer about themselves

Arrange to show around [ ]

Put on backup list [ ]

Not suitable [ ]

Sample letter to insurance company

Daffodil Cottage
Keswick
Cumbria

To: The Stardust Insurance Company
Stargazers Lane
London EC1

1 September 2001

From William Wordsworth

Dear Sirs

Policy No: WW/212/SGP/890/2

I have the above Property/the Contents of the above
Property [you will need to write separately to the
insurers of both the buildings and the contents if there
are two different insurance companies involved]
insured with you under the above policy.

I would like to inform you that I want to take in a
lodger. Will you please confirm that my
property/contents insurance will continue in full force
and effect during the letting, and that I will be fully
insured in the event of: damage to property [contents]
by my lodger or my lodger's visitors, theft of contents

by my lodger or my lodger's visitors, injury or death of my lodger or damage to my lodger's belongings caused by defects in my property [contents].

I should also like your assurance that my existing third party cover will also extend to my lodger.

I would be grateful for your early reply and thank you in anticipation of your kind assistance.

Yours faithfully

William Wordsworth

Sample reference request

Daffodil Cottage
Keswick
Cumbria

To: Mr P B Shelley
12 Skylark Rise
Crawley
Surrey

1 September 2001

Dear Sir,

I am considering taking in Mr Leigh Hunt as a lodger.
Mr Hunt has given your name as a referee. I should be
grateful if you would kindly tell me how long you have
known him and in what capacity and let me have your
views on his suitability as a lodger, including his ability
to pay the rent and to keep my property in good order.

I thank you in anticipation of your assistance in this
matter and attach a stamped, addressed envelope for
your reply.

Yours faithfully,

William Wordsworth

Sample receipt for rent

Date: 1 November 2001

Landlord: John Keats

Property address: Endymion House
                     Nightingale Way
                     St Agnes, Cornwall

Lodger: Sam Coleridge

Amount: £300

Period: 1 November to 30 November 2001

I acknowledge receipt of the amount above which is rent for the above period.

Landlord's Signature ....

Sample receipt for deposit

Date: 1 November 2001

Landlord: John Keats

Property address: Endymion House
                        Nightingale Way
                        St Agnes, Cornwall

Lodger: Sam Coleridge

Amount: £300

I acknowledge receipt of the amount above as deposit
that I agree to hold on the terms of the Lodger
Agreement between us of today's date.

Landlord's Signature ....

Sample rent demand

Date: 1 November 2001

Landlord: John Keats

Landlord's address: Endymion House
                                            Nightingale Way
                                            St Agnes, Cornwall

Lodger: Sam Coleridge

Amount: £300

Please make immediate payment of the amount stated above which is rent for the above period. Thank you.

Landlord's Signature ....

Your inventory

This inventory lists all the items in a spacious bed-
sitting room with a kitchen area and its own bathroom,
on the top floor of a large house. It is a ridiculously
comprehensive inventory. Do not be alarmed. Few
landlords would equip their lodger's accommodation,
especially the kitchen, so generously, but I have tried to
think of everything that you might consider supplying,
rather than miss anything out. You will wish to use my
inventory as an *aide mémoire* rather than as an
instruction to go out and buy your lodger a pizza cutter.
Delete anything you are not providing – and add
anything extra to the list.

It is a good idea to specify the manufacturer of major
items. I know a landlord whose lodger quietly swapped
the microwave for an inferior model and took the
expensive one away with her!

Always check electrical appliances before putting them
on the inventory. If it doesn't work reliably, you must
repair or replace it. Always include instruction manuals
in the inventory. If you have lost the instructions for
something, it is worth contacting the manufacturer and
asking for a fresh copy.

Remember to state the decorative condition of the
accommodation and to add wording such as 'All items
new or in very good condition unless otherwise stated'.

Your inventory should draw attention to anything that is shabby or damaged (the scorched carpet and discoloured Pyrex roasting dish, for example), so that nobody can blame the damage on your lodger.

Then print out two copies, one for you and one for your lodger.

Inventory

All items new or in very good condition unless otherwise stated

Kitchen area

Newly decorated

[Vinyl] flooring
[Strip] light fittings
[Slate grey] worktops
[   ] window blind
1 Zanussi washer/dryer
Instructions for same
1 sink unit with stainless steel sink
1 [Philips] [electric] cooker
Instructions for same
1 electric cooker hood
Instructions for same
1 [Whirlpool] fridge-freezer
Instructions for same
1 [Matsui] microwave cooker [with oven, grill and defrosting facilities]

Instructions for same
[ ] wall cupboards
[ ] low cupboards
[ ] drawer units containing
[ ] teaspoons
[ ] dessert spoons
[ ] dessert forks
[ ] table forks
[ ] large knives
[ ] small knives
[ ] serving spoons
1 apple corer
1 potato peeler
1 egg whisk
[ ] wooden spoons
[ ] spatulas
1 pair of tongs
1 potato masher
1 pizza cutter
1 pastry brush
1 pair of scissors
1 fish slice
1 bottle brush
1 strainer
1 grapefruit knife
1 cook's knife
1 paring knife
1 grater
1 perforated spoon
1 can opener
1 corkscrew
1 [Morphy Richards] electric kettle

Instructions for same
1 saucepan rack with:
1 milk pan
1 large metal saucepan + lid
1 glass large saucepan + lid
1 glass small saucepan; no lid

1 grill pan with holder
1 non-stick frying pan

1 wall clock
1 vegetable rack
1 breakfast bar
[ ] stools
1 large waste bin

1 electric slow cooker
Instructions for same
1 [terracotta] coffee jar
1 set of [ ] [terracotta] storage jars
1 stand for kitchen roll
[ ] trays
1 mug tree with [ ] mugs on it
1 [white china] teapot
[ ] table mats
1 colander
1 plastic jug
1 coffee pot; [ ] filter cones; 1 packet of filter papers
[ ] plastic canister
1 [Pyrex] roasting dish [discoloured but sound]
[ ] tumblers
1 salt & pepper set

1 measuring jug
[ ] large dinner plates
[ ] small plates
[ ] bowls
1 washing up bowl
1 bucket
1 dustpan and brush
1 [Hoover upright] vacuum cleaner with tools
Instructions for same
1 packet spare vacuum cleaner bags
[ ] dusters
1 squeegee mop

Bathroom

Newly decorated

[Vinyl] flooring
1 [pendant] light fitting with shade
1 strip light over wash basin 1 bath with shower
attachment
1 non-slip rubber bathmat
1 cotton bathmat
1 shower curtain and rail
1 lavatory [with pine seat]
1 wash basin
1 mirror
1 waste paper bin
1 bath mat
1 set of scales
1 toilet roll holder
1 lavatory brush

1 shelf
1 linen bin
1 wall heater
1 soap dish
1 extractor fan

Bed-sitting room

Newly decorated

1 fitted carpet [slight scorch mark near window]
1 pendant light fitting with shade
1 [double] bed
1 [metal action] sofa bed
1 [Flokati] rug
[ ] scatter cushions
[ ] pairs of [Sanderson Country Trail cotton] curtains
[plus matching tie backs]
1 dining table
[ ] dining chairs [with Sanderson Country Trail cotton
seat cushions]
[ ] bookcases
1 desk
1 table lamp
1 typist's chair
1 coffee table
[ ] armchairs
1 [Philips] TV and stand
Instructions for same
[ ] chests of drawers
1 waste paper bin
1 [electric storage] heater

Instructions for same
[ ] pictures
1 fitted wardrobe with shelves, containing:
1 duvet
[ ] pillows
[ ] duvet covers
[ ] bottom sheets
[ ] pillowslips
[ ] large towels
[ ] small towels

We have thoroughly checked this inventory and agree
that all is as set out above.

Signed ....**Lodger**

Signed ....**Landlord**

Date ....

Useful Contacts

DETR Free Literature
PO Box 236
Wetherby LS23 7NB

Telephone: 0870 1226 236

Fax: 0870 1226 237

Leaflets from the Inland Revenue
>www.inlandrevenue.gov.uk<

CORGI – Council of Registered Gas Installers
Helpline 01256 372300
>www.corgi-gas.com<

Index

Printed in the United Kingdom by The Stationery Office Ltd, London
TJ005101   C30   09/01   647047   19584